TRUCKING COMPANY

OWNER OPERATOR

VOLUME 1

BY ANDRE ERVING

MORE BY ANDRE ERVING

TRANSPORTATION BROKERAGE: FORMATION (VOLUME 1)

TRANSPORTATION BROKERAGE: OPERATION (VOLUME 2)

TRANSPORTATION BROKERAGE: SCALE (VOLUME 3)

TRUCKING COMPANY: OWNER OPERATOR (VOLUME 1)

TRUCKING COMPANY: OPERATION (VOLUME 2)

TRUCKING COMPANY: SCALE (VOLUME 3)

BUSINESS STRATEGY:

THE CEO YOU WANT TO BE (VOLUME 1)

20 STEPS TO SCALE YOUR BUSINESS

TRUCKING COMPANY

OWNER OPERATOR

VOLUME 1

TRUCKING COMPANY

OWNER OPERATOR

VOLUME 1

ANDRE ERVING

Erving's Publishing, LLC / Georgia

Erving's Publishing, LLC

3280 Pointe Parkway Ste 2000

Peachtree Corners, GA 30092

Copyright © 2023 by Andre Erving

All Rights Reserved

Printed in the United States of America

TABLE OF CONTENTS

CHAPTER 1 – BUSINESS FORMATION

HOW TO CHOOSE A BUSINESS NAME 15
HOW TO CHOOSE A BUSINESS STRUCTURE 15
WHAT IS TAX CLASSIFICATION? 17
SHOULD YOU GET A REGISTERED AGENT? 18
WHAT IS A REGISTERED AGENT? 18
WHERE ARE YOU CONDUCTING BUSINESS? 18
DO YOU NEED INSURANCE? 19
CITY, STATE, OR COUNTY LICENSING? 20
PROTECT YOUR BUSINESS NAME? 20
WHAT LEGAL DOCUMENTS ARE NEEDED? 21
DUN AND BRADSTREET NUMBER? 22
BUSINESS BANK ACCOUNT? 22

CHAPTER 2 – OBTAINING A TRUCK

WHAT TYPE OF TRUCK SHOULD I GET? 24
WHERE DO I GET A TRUCK FROM? 24
SHOULD I GET A USED OR A NEW TRUCK? 26
SHOULD I PAY CASH, RENT, OR LEASE? 26
SHOULD I PURCHASE A WARRANTY? 26
WHAT SHOULD BE INCLUDED? 27
WHAT TYPE OF INSURANCE DO I NEED? 27
WHERE ARE YOU GOING TO PARK? 28
EXPERIENCE TO OBTAIN INSURANCE? 29
DO I NEED A CDL OR A REGULAR LICENSE? 30
PAPERWORK THAT COMES WITH THE TRUCK? ...30

CHAPTER 3 – OBTAINING A TRAILER

WHAT TYPE OF TRAILER SHOULD I GET? 33
SHOULD I GET A USED OR NEW TRAILER? 33
DO I NEED INSURANCE? 33
SHOULD I PURCHASE A WARRANTY? 33
WHERE ARE YOU GOING TO PARK? 33
PAPERWORK THAT COMES WITH THE TRAILER? 34

CHAPTER 4 – OPERATOR AUTHORITY

WHAT IS OPERATOR AUTHORITY? 36
WHAT TYPE DO YOU NEED? 36
HOW MUCH DOES IT COST? 36
WHAT ARE THE REQUIREMENTS? 36
COMPLETE THE APPLICATION 36
WHAT WILL YOU HAUL? 37
WHERE WILL YOU HAUL? 37
WHERE CAN YOU HAUL? 37
HOW LONG DOES IT TAKE TO BECOME ACTIVE? 37

CHAPTER 5 – TRUCK & TRAILER REGISTRATION

REGISTER MY TRUCK AND TRAILER IN? 39
WHAT DOCUMENTS DO I NEED? 39
WHAT STATES DO I HAVE TO REGISTER IN? 39
WHAT IS IFTA? 39
WHAT IS IRP? 40
WHAT IS HVUT 2290?? 40

CONCLUSION

CONCLUSION 41

TRUCKING COMPANY

OWNER OPERATOR

VOLUME 1

INTRODUCTION

Andre Erving, A business expert that has built his career by helping others build and grow theirs. He started his career with a bachelor's degree in computer science and started doing IT work as an employee and doing contractor work on the side. He then started a computer repair business and sold it.

At that time, he decided to start a career in transportation by becoming a professional truck driver, this is where his knowledge in the trucking industry came from. He perfected his driving skills and became a professional truck driver trainer. This position consisted of training new drivers that had just received their Commercial Driver's License, also known as CDL, they would pair with a trainer, like Andre, for 30 to 45 days and learn how to operate a semi-truck while driving over the road.

After driving for 10 years, he obtained a semi-truck, became an owner-operator, and continued his career as a professional driver. On his journey as an owner-operator, he came across the term, Freight Broker, this was supposed to be the person an owner-operator would get their loads from. At this time another journey was created, that journey was to seek knowledge of what a Freight Broker is, what they do, and how to get in contact with one.

Andre started searching and found information on Freight Broker training, he reached out, learned how to broker, and became a Freight Broker Agent. He stopped driving for a couple of months so he could learn how to get his loads for his truck. He learned how to broker freight and started brokering on his own.

He started brokering so many loads that he never went back to driving his truck until after a year, yes, his truck is just sitting but brokering paid for it. Within a year of brokering, he got so good at it and created a simple online course on how to do it. He was still brokering, and people were starting to buy his course, so he decided to start a transportation brokerage.

This gave him more options and flexibility to train people and enabled him to switch his customers from the current brokerage he was with and over to his brokerage. He now has the platform to show people exactly how to broker freight using his customers from his brokerage. His brokerage is growing, and his online course sales are up, now he has decided to obtain office space and train people in person on how to broker freight.

While constantly growing, he opened another location for in-person training, he has 3000 students at that time, so he always has another journey he is on. He plans to open more locations throughout the USA, and he wants to open a location in Vancouver, British Columbia, Canada. While on these journeys, Andre became an author and started writing books, his first book was the Freight Broker Training manual that he gave away with his courses.

Since then, he has written 8 books including this one. Andre has traveled many journeys, while in the process, he obtained a bachelor's degree in business and a master's degree in business. So, 3 or 4 years have passed, and he decided not to get back in the truck; yes, now he decides this after the truck has been sitting all this time.

His vision is now in another direction, he doesn't have to drive anymore, so he decides to hire a driver, start a Trucking Company, and scale it.

In this book, I am going to teach you how to start a business and become an owner-operator

Read this book as a question-and-answer approach, that way it will keep you engaged

CHAPTER 1 – BUSINESS FORMATION

How to choose a business name. When choosing a business name, you want to think of a name that can scale with your business. Look at the future of your business, look at what you're trying to do with your business. If you want to scale your business properly, you will want to have a great name that can follow the business as it grows.

Many people have names such as They Mad Now Transportation, I'm Lit Trucking, or Hater's Gunna Hate Xpress. Yes, it is your business, and you can name it whatever you want, but think about what a bank or an investor is going to say if you ask them for a loan. You must have a name that when people look at it, they'll say, okay, interesting, that's a good brand name.

This makes them want to know more about who the owner(s) of that company is, which will open doors for your business if people are inquiring about it. Your name should catch people's attention and it should be easy to remember. Your name is the number one thing that's going to attract people, businesses, partnerships, Investors, etc.

If you're starting the business by yourself, then you can name the business a part of your name, either your first name, your middle name, your last name, etc. This all goes with personal branding, as you grow, you can make changes as needed. Always try to look towards the future when you are thinking about business.

Of course, you will think about today, but you want to think about the future of the business, brand names such as Walmart, Amazon, and General Mills stick out when you hear them.

How to choose a business structure. When choosing a business structure, you must first consider how many people will be involved in the business, and again, where you are trying to take the business, moving forward. There are sole proprietorships, general partnerships, limited liability partnerships, limited partnerships, and limited liability companies and then you have the corporations, such as S Corporations or C Corporations. Different business entities have different tax advantages and disadvantages, and legal documents that need to be filed, different licensing that's required, etc.

Consulting with a small business attorney may be a good idea if you have many people involved in the business and if you want to get more details on which structure best fits your needs. A sole proprietorship is the most common structure that is formed but is not an actual business entity. You can start a business under that classification of sole proprietorship but everything concerning the business will fall on the business owner of that business, taxes, debts, lawsuits, etc.

I do not recommend using sole proprietorship because it uses your social security number, your personal information, and all your business information together. When you start using LLCs and corporations as a business structure you give yourself a little more security and you split your personal and business information. Say for instance, if you are driving your truck, you crash into someone and they want to sue you, they can come after your house, your car, your assets, etc. if you have your business set up as a sole proprietorship, or what if somebody slips and falls at your business location and they want compensation, they will only be able to come after the business if the business structure is set up properly if it is a sole proprietorship, they will come after everything you own and they will get it.

LLC is another common business entity to have, which is a limited liability company. A lot of people go this route for tax purposes, the LLC pays taxes through an individual income tax code instead of a corporate tax code. Corporations are also good, they have limited liability, for instance, the shareholders of the corporation are only liable for the money they put up for their investment, and their personal assets will not be affected.

If your company has investors and you pay out profits to investors, you will pay them in a form of dividends, so they will be taxed on the money you gave them, and the business will be taxed on the money the business earned, this is called double taxation, LLCs do not get doubled taxed. Many people choose LLC because that's pretty much what they know about or have heard a lot about. Corporations are good for obtaining capital quickly, business security, and personal liability protection.

LLCs are good for flow-through taxation, and appreciating assets, such as intellectual property and real estate, they also have better flexibility for management. How the business is taxed is the main thing most people think about, if you are making serious money, you do not want to give it away in taxes. **What is a tax classification?** This is a category the IRS puts your business in when you apply for an EIN, which is short for Employer Identification Number.

If a business has at least two members, you can choose to be classified as either a taxable corporation or a partnership. If a business has a single member, it can choose to be classified as a taxable corporation or a disregarded entity from the business owner(s). You will be to see these options and other information related to obtaining an EIN during the process of completing the application.

You can only complete the application online during the week, during business hours, you will receive your EIN the same day. You may also complete the PDF document which is available online and mail it or fax it in, you can call the IRS as well to complete the application over the phone. Either option you choose, you will need your social security number, information about the business, the owners, and the address.

They will also ask what exactly the business is going to be doing, do you plan to hire employees and expect to pay your employment tax liability to be $1000 or less, and if you will be running a gambling facility to name a few. **Should you get a registered agent?** Yes, you should get a registered agent for your business. You can be the registered agent, or you can hire someone to be the registered agent.

What is a registered agent? A registered agent is a person or company that receives legal documents on behalf of a company or person. They must have a physical office in the same state that you have your business registered in. A registered agent is a good way to keep your business private. If you do not have a registered agent, you will have to enter your personal information and register yourself as a registered agent.

Once you register yourself, all your information is public, the registered agent will replace all your information with their information. It is a good idea to hire a registered agent before registering your business with the secretary of the state office. When you complete the application and you come to the part about registered agents, you will enter the registered agent's information you have received after purchasing their services.

Hiring a registered agent service varies in pricing, with many starting at $50 per year, but I have seen many that charge $400 per year depending on the type of company it is and the services they provide. You would have to get a registered agent for every business that you register with the secretary of the state office. **Where are you going to conduct business?** Is this going to be a home-based business, are you going to rent out office space, or are you going to purchase some property?

You might say, well, I'm going to be a truck driver, I'm not going to conduct business anywhere except in my truck. If you are just starting this might be the case, but don't forget to think about the future of your business, you want the business to scale, so obtaining office space might be a good idea early on. Even though you're driving the truck now, you might want to come out of the truck and bring on other owner-operators.

I go into more detail on this in my book called, Trucking Company: Scale (Volume 3). What if you want to hire a driver manager to manage your loads and book you on other loads? I go into detail on this in my book called, Trucking Company: Operation (Volume 2). These are things to consider early on when starting a company, this is called forward thinking. Bottom line is that you will need a space to operate that one truck, even if it's a space in your apartment or somewhere in your house.

You will need someone that is strictly dedicated to you that can help you grow, like an employee, wife, son, daughter, etc., not a random person that you met on the internet. You want that person to come to your office space and work for you every day, this is how you grow, by building a team from scratch. Always set your business up as if you have 100 or more employees for example, even though you don't have any or just one.

Do you need insurance? Yes, you will need insurance even if you have a home-based business or office space. Depending on the state you are in, they will have different insurance requirements. The most common will be business owner insurance or BOP (Business Owner Policy), this will give you general liability for the business, and it will give you property insurance for your property that's inside of the business.

You need general liability just in case it is a fire, or it floods, or somebody slips and falls, your general liability will cover this, a $1,000,000 (1 million dollar) policy is normal. What if somebody breaks into your place and steals two TVs, a microwave, and six computers, your property insurance will cover this, and you will obtain a policy that will insure all your property in case of damage or theft, such as a $40,000 (forty thousand dollar) insurance policy on your property. Some states require you to have at least a business owner policy, if you have a home-based business, you may be able to obtain insurance from the company you have insurance with already for your house.

You also want to think about professional liability insurance, this is insurance just in case you miss up while providing a service and you get sued, the professional liability will cover you for mistakes that you made. Remember, we are thinking ahead, so the more prepared you are in the beginning, the faster you can correct if something was to happen. **Do you need city, state, or county licensing?** Some states do not require a business license for a home-based business, I recommend checking with your state, city, and county professional licensing departments to inquire about licensing for your business.

More than likely, you will need a city business license for a trucking company whether it is home-based or office space. Some city licensing starts at $30 (thirty dollars), some are $250 (two-hundred fifty dollars), etc.

How do you protect your business name? Once you decide on a name for your business, it would be a good idea to see if someone else has the same name, if they do, you can check to see if that name has a trademark on it.

https://trademarks.justia.com/

If the name does have a trademark on it, you are prohibited from using that name nationwide if you use it in the same category as the other company, and you will have to choose another name. Trademarks do not expire if you keep the registration active, the owners must show proof that they are using the trademark in commerce. The United States Patent and Trademark Office grants trademarks and they might audit and or dismiss your trademark if you do not continue to provide valid proof that you are using it.

There are a lot of small businesses that have the same name and operate in the same industry, but they are registered in different states. If the name is not trademarked, you can register the name XYZ Trucking, LLC in Georgia, and register XYZ Trucking, LLC in Florida, for example. If XYZ Trucking has a trademark on it, nobody can use that name nationwide if they use it for transportation. You may learn more about trademarks by visiting https://www.uspto.gov/.

What legal documents are needed for your business? The basic legal documents that are needed are as follows: 1. The Articles of Operation for an LLC, or the Articles of Incorporation for a Corporation. 2. an Employer Identification Number or EIN Number, which will be provided to you on a document when you apply for your EIN. Your EIN Number is your business social security number. 3. a W9 form, which will be a document that you complete and give to customers that you're doing business with. A W9 form is used to file an information return with the IRS on the money that was paid to you from a business, or money you paid to a business. If you paid a business $600 (Six Hundred) or more, or they paid you $600 (Six Hundred) or more, both companies must file a W9 form for the money that was paid to the business.

Optional Documents are as follows: 4. Business License – If your state requires you to have a business license. 5. Business Owner Policy Insurance, which comes with general liability and property insurance – If your state requires you to have business owner policy insurance. 6. Trademark registration.

What is a Dun and Bradstreet number? Dun & Bradstreet is one of the leading suppliers of business information, they have a global database that contains commercial data on more than 200 million companies. Dun & Bradstreet holds the largest volume of business credit information as well, so if you are building business credit, you might want to sign up for a D&B Number, this will be your business credit profile number. A lot of companies require you to have a Dun & Bradstreet number before they conduct business with you. They want to look at your company's business credit profile before they decide to do business with your company. You may learn more at https://www.dnb.com/

What do I need to get a business bank account?

The items that are needed are as follows: 1. Your Social Security Card, you may be able to use a Passport as well. 2. Your State ID or Driver's License. 3. The Articles of Operation for an LLC, or the Articles of Incorporation for a Corporation. 4. Your Employer Identification Number or EIN Number document. 5. A W9 form. 6. All the owners of the business that own 25% or more of the company must be present to sign the required documents to open an account. Some banks will let the owners come in at different times to sign, or depending on the bank, they might send the owners a DocuSign link in the email to sign. The account cannot be opened until all the owners sign all the required documents.

CHAPTER 2 – OBTAINING A TRUCK

What type of truck should I get? You should get the truck that best fits your needs for your business, but I recommend getting a semi-tractor and a trailer. If you're going to do this, you might as well go for the goal. A lot of people think they should get a straight truck or a box truck and try to run it like a semi-truck operation. A straight truck or box truck is for companies that manufacture products and provide delivery services to their customers.

A box truck is not for someone to purchase and try and call themselves an owner-operator with that one truck. They will have a hard time finding loads to haul. Those loads only pay $1 (one dollar), $1.50 (one dollar fifty) per mile. So, if you waste 10k putting down on a straight truck or a box truck, you won't make enough money to cover the expenses for the truck every month and receive profit for yourself.

You will have truck insurance, cargo insurance, truck payment, fuel, and a load board, and you will result to using quick pay and a factoring company to receive your money quickly. These options will take a percentage of your profit. If you do find a load going somewhere, how will you find a load getting back? Purchasing a straight truck or box truck will limit you to only hauling LTL (less than truckload) freight. I go over this more in detail in my Trucking Company: Operation (Volume 2) book.

Where do I get a truck from? There are many places to purchase trucks, and that is the tricky part about it. When you get a truck, you want to make sure that you are getting it from a place that lets you use your EIN. A lot of places want you to purchase trucks by using your social security number, one reason is to hold you 100% liable for the truck should something happen. But when you are doing business, you should not put your social security number on anything except a bank account, a credit card, or a line of credit, everything else should use your EIN.

Depending on the company, your business credit, and what you are trying to get, a company might ask you to list yourself, someone else, or another business as a personal guarantee. A personal guarantee will state that no matter what happens or whatever situation it is, the bill is still going to get paid, you can say this is something like a co-signer. I recommend getting a truck from a leasing company that specializes in leasing trucks to businesses, and not just individuals. Remember, you are trying to start a business and scale it, so you need to be able to add trucks to your fleet using your business credentials.

This will also help build your business credit when you pay the truck note, pay the truck off, and add more trucks to your fleet. I go over this in detail in my Trucking Company: Scale (Volume 3) book. As of right now, there are many places available to get trucks with $3500 (thirty-five hundred) or $5,000 (five thousand) down, you can do a Google search for semi-truck leasing, and you will find many trucks available. If you do not have experience with truck parts, tune-ups, tires, etc., I recommend finding someone who does before you lease or purchase a truck.

If you lease or purchase a truck, I recommend getting something no more than 3 to 5 years old. The older your truck is the higher the insurance premium is going to be in some cases because the truck is a liability. You also don't want to be in the shop every week because something went wrong either, if the wheels are not moving, no money is being made, and roadside assistance and getting a tow truck is expensive as well. Newer trucks have high insurance premiums also, but you will not be in the shop as much because the truck is fairly new.

[LRM Leasing](#) and [OTR Leasing](#) are a couple of places that will let you lease trucks using your EIN.

Should I get a used or a new truck? When you're just starting, I recommend getting a used truck unless you can afford to buy or lease a brand-new truck. There will be a $20,000 (twenty thousand) or more down payment for a new truck, and a $10,000 (ten thousand) or less down payment for a used truck. You do not want to start a business with high debt after the business has started. You will wreck your brain trying to pay a $5000 (five thousand) per month truck note when you should be focused on growing the business.

When you build a relationship with the dealership and you add more trucks to your fleet, your payments will go lower. When your business establishes business credit, you will walk out with 3 to 5 trucks with no money down. Therefore, you must get a Dun & Bradstreet number and use your EIN for everything, this will help you build your business credit. New trucks are running for $200,000 (two hundred thousand) right now before financing, a good used truck is running for around $40,000 (forty thousand) and up before financing.

Should I pay cash, rent, or lease? If you can pay cash upfront for a truck, I recommend doing that, you will only have to pay the insurance and keep the maintenance up. I do not recommend renting a truck unless your truck is in the shop, it costs upward of $1000 (one thousand) per week, plus mileage to rent a truck. If you are on a budget or do not want to cash for a truck, then I recommend leasing a truck until you can build your capital and business credit.

Should I purchase a warranty? If you purchase or lease a truck it should come with a warranty out the door, even if it is a warranty for 1 or 2 months. You should have some type of grace period for repairs, or you should be able to bring it back before a certain time if you don't want it. Some places have a 72-hour grace period to bring the truck back if something happens, others have 30 days, etc. Therefore, you should get a warranty before you drive off the lot, if possible, at the time, get a warranty from another company.

Usually, warranties from the dealer do not cover everything, it is just something to hush your mouth so you can buy the truck and go. If you purchase the warranty from somewhere else, you might have a better chance of getting the entire truck covered with the engine, trans, DPF, injectors, extended mileage, etc., all included in one low monthly price, some places charge a one-time fee as well. You can get a warranty for $3,500 (three thousand five hundred) or more, this will depend on many factors. I have seen dealer warranties for 10,000 (ten thousand) miles or 2 months, whichever comes first, and it only covers cosmetic parts, which will be all the parts that are attached to the engine and throughout the truck, but no warranty on the engine itself or the transmission.

The dealer's job is to sell trucks, not pay out money for a truck they sold for $50,000 (fifty thousand), they will be losing on that deal. So, getting a warranty from another provider will be a smart thing to do. **What should be**

included in the warranty? There are many things to take into consideration when you purchase a warranty, so you must read it carefully and make sure that it includes everything you want, or at least most of it. You want to make sure the warranty covers your engine, transmission, fuel pump, engine control module, water pump, turbocharger, Exhaust Gas Recirculation valves and cooler, Aftertreatment Electronic Control Module, DPF module, etc., the list goes on, I just named a few. Again, you want your warranty to include almost everything that could go wrong on the truck, if not all things.

So, you may have to search around a bit so you can get a good warranty, but it will be worth it when something happens. **What type of insurance do I need?** The Federal Motor Carrier Safety Administration (FMCSA) requires all commercial vehicles over 10,001 (ten thousand one) LBS (pounds) to obtain a minimum of $750,000 (seven hundred fifty thousand) Bodily, Injury, and Property Damage insurance, and a minimum of $100,000 (one hundred thousand) contingent cargo insurance if you have a trailer. Many people just get $1,000,000 (one million) worth of insurance.

Many customers require $1,000,000 (one million) of insurance, so it's best to just go ahead and get it from the beginning. The $100,000 (one hundred thousand) Contingent Cargo Insurance is insurance for the cargo that is inside the trailer. Many customers require $1,000,000 (one million) or more insurance as well, depending on the products they are shipping.

Where are you going to park the truck? Many people forget about this until the insurance company asks where the truck will be parked. They ask this question because this is one of the factors they are going to use to calculate your monthly premium. If you park your truck outside on the street, your assurance is going to be higher, if you park your truck on a secured lot with a gate around it, then your insurance is going to be cheaper. They will also base your premium on what city the truck will be parked in. There are many places around where you can park your truck for $150 (one hundred fifty) or $200 (two hundred) bucks per month on a secured lot.

    You can search google for truck parking near your location and you will see many places available that you didn't know existed. Many guys with day cabs park their trucks on the street, in their backyards, or somewhere else around the neighborhood because they are local drivers. I still recommend parking your truck in a secure lot, I parked my truck on the street one time, and I came out and someone crashed into the back of it and the side and kept going of course. This ruined my whole day, that's how I found out about $1000 (one thousand) or more per week for truck rentals.

    You will have to pay a deductible to get the truck fixed and pay $1000 (one thousand) or more per week for a truck rental, and depending on your deductible, this may ruin your profit for around 4 months or more because you have to work to get that money back. What if your truck is in the shop, you have a rental truck, and the rental truck has a tire blowout, or the truck shuts off while you are driving and you have to call road service and they have you waiting for 4 hours before they come out, and you are you under a load? Oh, I have many stories for you!

Now you have more money to spend, and you just spent $3000 (three thousand) for a deductible and $1000 (one thousand) or more to get the rental truck. Expenses will add up quickly is what I am saying, and problems usually happen back-to-back, so don't create more problems for yourself. I recommend finding a secure lot and parking your truck there, you will have a better chance of staying stress-free.

Do I need any experience to obtain insurance?
You do not need to have any experience to obtain

insurance, but how high or low your insurance premium is will depend on how much experience you have. This is why a lot of companies say you need two years or more of experience to drive for them because insurance will be lower for you, it was not your driving record; they did not want to pay $40,000 (forty thousand) per year to get an insurance policy on you. The mega carriers will hire you with no experience because most of them own their own insurance company.

When you are an owner-operator you will have no choice but to pay $3000 (three thousand) per month for insurance if they tell you that. This is another reason why most owner-operators go out of business; the insurance is too high. They result in leasing their truck to a company like JB Hunt, Schneider, etc., and run under that company's authority.

When you call an insurance company to get a quote, they're going to ask for your MVR report, if you don't have it ready to email it to them, they are going to ask for your consent to run your MVR right there over the phone, they are going to ask for your CDL number, they are going to ask where are you going to park the truck, how much experience do you have, do you have a trailer, how much insurance do you need, what state is the truck registered in and any other questions they may have to qualify you.

Insurance companies will usually quote you around $20,000 (twenty thousand) for the year, but I have seen quotes for 40 (forty) and $50,000 (fifty thousand) for one year. **Do I need a CDL or a regular license?** If your truck weighs more than 26,001 (twenty-six thousand one) LBS (pounds), or more than 10,001 (ten thousand one) LBS (pounds) if you tow a car, you are required to have a Commercial Driver's License or CDL.

What type of paperwork comes with the truck? When leasing or purchasing a truck you will have to sign many documents. After completion, you will receive the documents below: 1. temporary registration, 2. temporary title with the leasing company as the owner and they will put you down as the lessee, 3. a bill of sale, 4. a copy of the pm or preventative maintenance report of all the work that was done on the truck, most people call it a DOT, if they do not show and provide you with a copy of this report, do not purchase the truck. You will need those documents for future repairs so you can know what to fix, what was fixed, etc. A lot of insurance and warranty companies will ask for this document as well, depending on the situation. 5. the lease agreement, which will be many documents, 5. a temporary plate or a trip permit so you can drive the truck to its destination, you must get a trip permit in each state that you will drive through while taking the truck to its destination, they are usually 72-hour permits, and 6. all other documents the company wants you to have concerning the truck or agreements that have been made.

You want to make sure you have these documents before you leave just in case you get stopped by the state troopers on the way driving the truck to its destination, do not forget your $750,000 (seven hundred fifty thousand) insurance either. Once you get the truck from the leasing company, dealer, etc., you must take the truck to your secure lot and leave it there until you register it with the state you set your business up in. A lot of people hang the temporary plate in the front window of the truck on the right side.

CHAPTER 3 – OBTAINING A TRAILER

What type of trailer should I get? It all depends on what type of freight you want to haul; I recommend getting a dry van trailer when you are just starting until you learn the business, then get another kind of trailer. If you want to get more money, you can get a refrigerated trailer, and if you like to work out a little, then you can get a flatbed trailer. **Should I get a used or new trailer?** You have a few options for trailers, yes you want to get a good trailer that's going to hold up for a while, same as with a truck, but right now, you can rent a trailer for around $1200 (twelve hundred) per month.

If you want to purchase one, you can lease one, for about 5 (five) or $600 (six hundred) per month depending on the type of trailer. If you don't get approved for one, you can always rent one for around $1000 (one thousand) per month until you can save around $7000 (seven thousand) or more to buy one. **Do I need insurance?** Yes, you will need insurance for your trailer, it is going to be based on the year of the trailer and how much insurance you want. You will more than likely get the trailer insurance from the same place you got the truck insurance.

Sometimes it will be cheaper to add both at the time if you have the trailer when you get the truck. Sometimes it might be cheaper to purchase insurance separately, so search around for better quotes before you make a decision. **Should I purchase a warranty?** Yes, you should purchase a warranty for the trailer as well. As I stated earlier, it might be best to purchase a warranty from another company, things happen with the trailers, so you want to be prepared.

Where are you going to park the trailer?
More than likely, you're going to park at the same place as you park the truck. But if you are not going to park in the same place, then you must figure out where you're going to park the trailer. Insurance is going to be based on where the trailer is parked just

like with insurance on the truck. If you have your truck and trailer registered in one state, and you're going to have the truck and trailer parked in another state, the insurance may get higher as well.

What paperwork do you need for the trailer? Your trailer will come with many documents as well. 1. the title for the trailer if you purchase it, and a temporary title with the dealer at the owner, and you as the lessee, 2. A warranty should come with the trailer, but many trailers are sold as is, if this is the case, I would purchase a warranty from another company before I leave the lot, 3. A report of all the repairs and maintenance that was done on the trailer, this is called a PM or Preventive Maintenance report, or a DOT report on the trailer, 4. A bill of sale, 5. Temporary registration, 6. any other documents or agreements the dealer has for the trailer. Do not forget your insurance either.

CHAPTER 4 – OPERATOR AUTHORITY

What is operator authority? Operator authority is the authority to operate a commercial vehicle. This authority comes from fulfilling the requirements of the FMCSA, which stands for the Federal Motor Carrier Safety Administration, an agency within the United States Department of Transportation. You must apply for operator authority and pay a fee, and authority will be granted by the FMCSA if you meet all the requirements.

What type of operator authority do you need? There are different types, so this depends on if you are going to stay intrastate, which means you only work in one state, or if you are going to go interstate, which means you are going to more than one state. The average owner-operator is going to apply for a regular common carrier operator authority, which will give you authority to operate in the entire USA. **How much does it cost?** Operating authority costs $300 (three hundred) and you can purchase this from the FMCSA website.

What are the requirements? There are a few tasks that must be completed before your operator authority will become active, the tasks to complete are as follows: 1. Complete the application for Operator Authority, first-time users must apply online at the FMCSA website, 2. Complete the application to file for BOC-3 Process Agents, the process agents will accept legal documents on your company's behalf in all 50 states, 3. A minimum of $750,000 (seven hundred fifty thousand) Bodily, Injury, Property Damage insurance, 4. A minimum of $100,000 (one hundred thousand) Cargo Insurance. You can search google for BIPD insurance and Cargo Insurance.

What do you need to complete the application? The tasks needed to complete the application are as follows: 1. You will need your EIN, 2. If you have a Dun & Bradstreet number you will be able to enter it, 3. your business name, 4. your business Address, P.O. Box numbers are not allowed, 5. your business phone number,

6. the number of drivers you will have, 7. the number of trailers you will have, 8. the number of trucks you will have, 9. the commodities you are going to haul, 10. the owner's information, and 11. $300 (three hundred), they do not provide refunds, so if you are skeptical, you may visit www.andreerving.com, pick a package, and have my team complete your project.

What will you haul? I recommend getting a dry van trailer in the beginning and hauling dry goods, which they call general freight. The FMCSA has requirements on what you can and cannot haul, based on the type of truck and trailer you have. They have a long list of items you can and cannot haul on their website. **Where will you haul?** I recommend hauling the entire USA, I have been to every state, a few times, and over the road is where the money is at, if you want to go home every night you are limiting yourself.

Where can you haul? As a common carrier, you can haul general freight anywhere in the USA, and haul freight to Mexico and Canada, if you do not have a contact in those countries to get a load from, you will have to use the load board to get a load back or just come back empty. Yes, you will be stopped and searched at the borders, and all your stuff must be squeaky clean, or you will be held up or stuck and can't come back until your stuff is verified. You will be told what you need before you book the load so you can have a heads-up, if you don't have what you need do not take the load.

A lot of people haul loads to the border and turn around and come back they don't go out of the country. **How long does it take to obtain operator authority?** It takes about 28 days to obtain operating authority if you have met all the requirements listed above.

CHAPTER 5 – TRUCK & TRAILER REGISTRATION

What state should I register my truck and trailer in? You can register your truck in any state you choose, I recommend looking at the registration fees in each state throughout the USA, and make your decision based on what you find. Keep in mind also about truck parking and insurance, you will also have to go to the registration office of that state to register in person, some states let you do this online as well. Here is a list of all the state fees in each state from the Federal Highway Administration.

What documents do I need to register my truck and trailer? The documents to register your truck with that state are as follows: **Truck** - 1. Temporary title with the dealership listed at the owner, and your business listed at the lessee, 2. bill of sale, 3. 2290 Form, 4. State ID or CDL, 5. International Registration Plan or IRP, 6. A minimum of $750,000 (seven-hundred fifty thousand) insurance policy, 7. International Fuel Tax Agreement or IFTA.

Trailer – 1. Temporary title with the dealership listed as the owner, and your business listed at the lessee, 2. bill of sale, 3. insurance, 4. State ID or CDL.

What states do I have to register my truck in? There are four states that require you to register your truck for highway use mileage, they are 1. Kentucky, 2. New Mexico, 3. New York, 4. Oregon. You will have to go to each state's website to register, some states let you purchase a temporary permit if you are traveling through the state often. Kentucky, New Mexico, New York, and Oregon.

What is IFTA? International Fuel Tax Agreement or IFTA – You must file this with the department of revenue in the state where you registered your business. This is a fuel tax that is collected by all commercial vehicles, it is for the redistribution of fuel taxes paid by interstate commercial carriers.

What is IRP? International Registration Plan or IRP – You must file for IRP for any vehicle that is over 26,000 (twenty-six thousand) LBS (pounds) and you cross states lines to move freight, filing your IRP will get you license plates, also known as Apportioned Plates

What is HVUT 2290? 2290 Form – If your truck is 55,000 (fifty-five thousand) LBS (pounds) or more, you will need to file a Highway Vehicle Use Tax form called 2290, you can file this form online or some states let you file it in person,

CONCLUSION

There are many pieces to bring together to start a business and become an owner-operator, I hope this book has left you with more knowledge than you came with. If you learned one thing from me, then this book was worth it. My goal was to teach you how to start a business and become an owner-operator. But this is the beginning, I have two more books about trucking for you to read so you can continue your journey.

Other Great Reads

Trucking Company: Operation (Volume 2)

Trucking Company: Scale (Volume 3)

Transportation Brokerage: Formation (Volume 1)

Transportation Brokerage: Operation (Volume 2)

Transportation Brokerage: Scale (Volume 3)

www.ingramcontent.com/pod-product-compliance
Lightning Source LLC
Chambersburg PA
CBHW031546210526

45464CB00003B/1175